CARING FOR LOVE BIRD

Pet Owners guide

A COMPLETE GUIDE TO KEEPING LOVEBIRDS AS PETS

DR MICK WALSH

Table of Contents

Introduction

Lovebirds are enchanting and endearing birds that have captured the hearts of bird watchers around the world. Lovebirds make amazing pets for those who are willing to give them the time and care they need. They are known for their bright colors, lively dispositions, and close relationships with their partners. We'll delve into the fascinating world of lovebirds in this comprehensive book, discovering their origins, species diversity, and the pleasures and responsibilities of owning them as treasured companions.

History and origins:

The Greek words "agape", meaning "love", and "ornis", meaning "bird", are the origins of the genus Agapornis, which includes lovebirds. These small parrots are native to Africa, where they can be found in savannahs, woodlands, and other types of habitats. Although the precise origin of the term "lovebird" is unknown, it is said to come from the strong, monogamous pair relationships that these birds develop.

For millennia, the history of lovebirds has been rich. Writings dating back to the 17th century first mention them, praising their endearing appearance and dedicated actions. During the colonial era, lovebirds were brought to various parts of the world by European explorers and traders, giving them enormous popularity as pets.

Species diversity:

There are nine species of lovebirds in the genus Agapornis, and each has distinct qualities and characteristics. These species are generally divided into two groups: the genus Agapornis, which includes the peach-faced, rosy-faced, Nyasa, red-headed, Abyssinian, and Malagasy lovebirds; and the genus Agapornis, which includes the masked, black-cheeked Fischer lovebirds.

The peach-faced lovebird (Agapornis roseicollis) is the most popular species in the pet trade and is kept in most homes. But because each species is unique in color, pattern, and temperament, lovers have a wide range of choices to choose from when choosing a lovebird companion.

The Entertaining Nature of Cupids:

Lovebirds' captivating personalities are among their most endearing traits. These tiny parrots are renowned for their lively antics, curious nature, and close emotional relationships with their human partners and guardians. Lovebirds make excellent pets for people looking for energetic and interesting companions, as they are very social creatures who thrive on interaction and companionship.

Additionally, lovebirds are well known for their melodic whistles, screams, and chirps. Lovebirds are not as good imitators as other larger parrot species, but with enough repetition and practice, they can learn to imitate particular vocalizations and sounds.

Their affectionate behaviors towards their human partners and companions are another endearing characteristic of lovebirds. Mutual feeding, preening, and even cuddling for warmth and comfort are some of their known behaviors. For many owners, one of the most satisfying things about owning lovebirds as pets is seeing these expressions of affection.

The binding process:

Establishing a strong bond with your partner is crucial to cultivating a relationship based on mutual trust and satisfaction. The bonding process, which requires patience, consistency and positive reinforcement, begins the moment you bring your lovebird home.

Start by spending time with your lovebird every day, engaging in calm, gentle interactions. Reward desired behaviors with incentives, including walking on your hand or perching on your shoulder. Your sweetheart will grow to adore you and form a strong sense of trust as he equates your presence with good things.

It is essential to respect your partner's boundaries and not pressure them in embarrassing circumstances. Let them come to you at their convenience, and never chastise or chastise them for showing signs of fear or hesitation. You can create a strong, lasting relationship with your romantic partner that will improve both of your lives by developing mutual respect and trust.

Lovebirds are incredibly fascinating animals that provide their hosts with happiness, companionship, and continued entertainment. Lovebirds have a unique way of winning the hearts of bird lovers everywhere, whether it's through their bright colors, vivacious personality, or loving nature.

Your lovebird will thrive if you give it the care and attention it needs and are aware of its origins, species diversity and distinctive traits. You can create a strong, lasting relationship with these endearing birds by being patient, persistent, and showing them true love. Why not experience this fascinating adventure with an inseparable friend and discover the pleasures of life together?

Chapter 1

Selecting the appropriate type of lovebird

For those interested in becoming bird owners, choosing the right species of lovebird is essential. With nine different species to choose from, each with particular qualities and attributes, it's important to take a number of things into account to ensure you and your feathered companion are a good match. We'll look at the different species of lovebirds, their behavioral and physical characteristics, and offer relevant information in this comprehensive guide to help you choose the best lovebird species for your needs.

- Recognize the diversity of lovebird species:

The genus Agapornis, which includes nine species native to different regions of Africa, includes lovebirds. These species can be broadly divided into two groups: the genus Agapornis, which includes the following species: Peach-faced Lovebird (Agapornis roseicollis), Rose-faced Lovebird (Agapornis roseicollis), Nyasa Lovebird (Agapornis lilianae), Red-headed Lovebird (Agapornis lilianae), Agapornis roseicollis). Agapornis pullarius), the Abyssinian Lovebird (Agapornis taranta) and the Madagascar Lovebird (Agapornis canus).

Because of their different colors, patterns, and behavioral characteristics, each species of lovebird is special and endearing in its own right. Understanding the distinctions between these species is essential in order to choose the ideal lovebird species based on your tastes, lifestyle, and level of experience as a bird owner.

- Physico-behavioral characteristics:

To ensure peaceful coexistence and suitable living conditions, it is crucial to take into account the physical and behavioral characteristics of the lovebird species you choose. Here are some essential qualities to consider:

Size: Lovebirds come in different sizes; some species are smaller and more delicate, while larger and more robust species are observed. For example, the peach-faced lovebird is one of the largest species, reaching a length of 6 to 7 inches, but the Fischer's lovebird is smaller, typically reaching a length of 5 to 6 inches.

Lovebirds are recognized for their eye-catching and colorful feathers, with each species displaying distinct patterns and color markings. For example, the masked lovebird is distinguished by a black mask on its face, while the peach-faced lovebird gets its name from its peach-colored face and bright green body.

Temperament: Different species and individuals of lovebirds may exhibit different personality traits. While some species, like the Black-cheeked Lovebird, can be quieter or reserved, others, like the Peach-faced Lovebird, are known for their gregarious and playful behavior.

Lovebirds are gregarious birds that use a range of vocalizations to communicate, such as whistles, squawks and chirps. When selecting a lovebird species, consider your noise tolerance since some may be more talkative than others.

Socialization: Lovebirds are gregarious birds that develop close relationships with their partners and human companions. Ask yourself if you have the time and means to give your lovebird the companionship and social engagement it needs to survive.

- Points to consider when selecting:

To ensure that you and your feathered companion are a good match, it is important to take into account a number of considerations when choosing the appropriate lovebird species. Here are some important points to remember:

Personal Preferences: Invest time in learning about different species of lovebirds, including their physical attributes and behavioral characteristics. Think about the species whose size, color, arrangement and vocalizations best suit your tastes.

Lifestyle and Living Arrangements: Evaluate your living situation and lifestyle to see if you have the time, money, or space to accept a lovebird. Consider things like your living space, your tolerance for noise, and any possible interactions with other pets.

Experience Level: When selecting a lovebird species, consider your level of experience as a bird owner. Some species might be better suited to novice bird owners, while others will be better suited to seasoned owners who are familiar with the needs and habits of lovebirds.

Compatibility: Consider whether a lovebird would fit well into your current household dynamic if you currently have other pets or if members of your family have allergies or sensitivities.

Breeding Considerations: To ensure happy partnerships and healthy offspring, if you are interested in breeding lovebirds, learn about the compatibility and breeding requirements of different species.

Selecting the ideal species of lovebird is an important choice that requires serious thought and investigation. You can make an informed choice that will lead to happy and rewarding companionship with your feathered friend by being aware of the wide variety of lovebird species, their physical and behavioral traits, as well as factors such as personal preferences, lifestyle and experience level. There is the ideal lovebird species just waiting to win your heart and improve your life, whether you are attracted to the bright colors of the peach-faced lovebird or the endearing behavior of the Fischer's lovebird .

Chapter 2

How to Create the Perfect Habitat for Your Lovebird: A Step-by-Step Guide to Creating a Safe and Interesting Space

Ensuring the health, happiness and overall well-being of your lovebird depends on creating the ideal habitat for them. Lovebirds are gregarious, energetic animals that do best in environments that provide plenty of space for enrichment, exercise, and excitement. The essential elements of creating the perfect habitat for your lovebird, such as choosing the right cage, where to place it, adding perches and accessories, improving the environment and taking safety precautions, will all be covered in detail in this book complete.

- Choose a cage:

Creating a safe and comfortable home for your lovebird starts with selecting the ideal cage. Consider the following aspects when choosing a cage:

Size: Choose a cage that gives your lovebird plenty of room to roam, spread its wings and exhibit its natural habits. For a single lovebird, a minimum required cage size of 24 inches long by 18 inches wide and 24 inches tall is suggested. However, larger cages are always better because they provide more room for mobility.

Bar Spacing: Make sure the distance between the cage bars is sufficient to prevent your lovebird from escaping or getting its head stuck between them. For lovebirds, optimal bar spacing is 1/2 to 5/8 inches.

Material: Choose a cage made of sturdy, non-toxic materials like powder-coated metal or stainless steel.

Avoid cages constructed of materials that may contain poisons or dangerous chemicals.

Accessibility: For easier cleaning and maintenance, choose a cage with multiple access doors and removable trays. This will make it easier to communicate with your lovebird and allow you to provide him with toys, fresh food and water.

- Cage position:

For the comfort, safety and general well-being of your lovebird, the location of its cage is essential. The following tips will help you choose the best location for your lovebird's cage:

Avoid drafts and direct sunlight: Place the cage away from drafts, very hot or cold temperatures and direct sunlight. Due to their sensitivity to temperature changes, lovebirds may feel anxious if they are around drafts or excessive heat.

Social Interaction: Place the cage in the middle of the house so your lovebird can see and interact with other family members as well as participate in daily events. This will encourage socialization and reduce feelings of isolation and loneliness.

Calm environment: To reduce stress and anxiety, place your lovebird's cage in a calm, serene corner of your home. Keep the cage away from televisions, loud appliances, and high-traffic areas.

Safety Considerations: To avoid any incidents or conflicts, make sure the cage is kept out of reach of other animals, such as dogs and cats. Stay away from the cage, keep away common household threats such as electrical cables, poisonous plants and household chemicals.

- Chairs and add-ons:

It is essential to provide your lovebird with a range of perches and accessories to keep them emotionally and physically engaged. The following should be part of your lovebird's habitat:

Natural wood perches: To promote good foot health and avoid foot problems, offer a range of natural wood perches of different diameters. Sandpaper and rough textured perches should not be used as they may cause abrasions and discomfort.

Enrichment toys and activities: To keep your sweetheart happy and engaged, provide a range of enrichment toys and activities. Toys that promote natural behaviors and mental stimulation include chew toys, bells, swings and ropes.

Choose food and water dishes that are securely attached to the cage and easy to clean and maintain. Place plates away from perches to avoid contaminating them with trash and droppings.

Nest Box: To create a secure and comfortable nesting area for your lovebirds, include a nest box in the cage if you intend to breed them. To meet the needs of breeding pairs, make sure the nest box is the right size and location.

- Environmental improvement:

To prevent your lovebird from getting bored, to stimulate his mind and to encourage natural behaviors, you must enrich his environment. The following tips can help you improve your lovebird's habitat:

Rotate Toys Often: To keep your lovebird interested and avoid boredom, rotate the toys you introduce to him frequently. Offer an assortment of hues, patterns and shapes to pique their curiosity and promote a hands-on experience.

Foraging Opportunities: To promote natural foraging behaviors in your lovebird, include toys and foraging activities in its daily routine. To provide mental and physical excitement, hide food and rewards in different areas of the cage.

Outdoor exposure: Give your sweetheart the opportunity to spend time outside in a safe, supervised setting when the weather permits. Exposure to daylight, fresh air, and external stimuli can improve your lovebird's overall health and provide essential enrichment.

- Safety observations:

Ensuring your lovebird's habitat is safe is essential to avoiding accidents, injuries and health problems. Here are some crucial safety factors to remember:

Non-toxic materials: Avoid products and materials that may contain poisons, dangerous chemicals or pesticides. To reduce the risk of chemical exposure, select bird-safe toys, cage accessories and cleaning products.

Safe perches and accessories: Check toys, cage accessories and perches frequently for wear or damage. As soon as something wears out or becomes damaged, replace it to avoid any accidents or injuries.

Hygiene and cleanliness: Constantly clean and disinfect the cage, perches, plates and toys to maintain a hygienic and clean environment. Every day, remove food scraps, dirty bedding and feces to stop the growth of bacteria and disease.

Monitoring and Supervision: Keep an eye on your lovebird every time he leaves his cage to avoid accidents or unsuccessful escape attempts. Check your lovebird's behavior, appetite and general health regularly. If you notice signs of illness or discomfort, consult a veterinarian.

Providing your lovebird with the ideal habitat is essential if you want to improve their overall well-being, happiness, and health. You can build a comfortable and stimulating living space that your lovebird will love by choosing a good cage, choosing the perfect location, providing a range of perches and accessories, enriching its environment and making sure it is safe at all times. To adapt to your lovebird's changing desires and preferences, remember to periodically evaluate and improve its habitat. You can also relish the rewarding experience of having a happy and healthy lovebird as a companion in your life.

chapter 3

Nutrition and Diet Guidelines

The health and well-being of your lovebird depends on a balanced diet. Essential vitamins, minerals and nutrients needed to maintain overall health, maintain a robust immune system and achieve longevity are found in a balanced diet. Lovebird feeding and nutrition standards will be covered in detail in this comprehensive guide, along with tips on creating healthy eating habits, food suggestions, and the value of a diverse diet.

- The value of a diverse diet

Like all parrots, lovebirds thrive on a broad, well-balanced diet rich in a variety of nutrient-dense foods. In addition to providing essential nutrients, a varied assortment of meals prevents food boredom and promotes natural foraging practices. Combinations of prepared pellets, fresh produce, grains and sometimes sweet treats can make up a diverse diet.

- Suggested meals for couples:

Created Pellets: A convenient and well-balanced way to give essential nutrients to lovebirds is to use premium pellets specially created for them. To support your lovebird's overall health, look for pellets enriched with vitamins, minerals and amino acids.

Fresh Fruits: Treat your sweetheart to an assortment of fresh fruits, including oranges, bananas, apples, strawberries and grapes. Fruits provide vital hydration and are an excellent source of vitamins, antioxidants and fiber. Before feeding fruit to your lovebird, be sure to remove any seeds, pits, or pits, as they can be toxic.

Vegetables: Include a range of fresh vegetables in your lovebird's diet, such as broccoli, squash, peppers, leafy greens and carrots. Vegetables are an excellent source of dietary fiber for digestive health and are also a powerful source of vitamins, minerals and antioxidants.

Grains and Legumes: Include cooked grains and legumes in your lovebird's diet, such as quinoa, rice, lentils, and beans. These foods can be served cooked or sprouted for increased nutritional benefit. They offer complex carbohydrates, proteins and important components.

Nuts and Seeds: Although you can give your lovebird occasional treats like seeds and nuts, they should not make up the majority of his diet. To avoid weight and nutritional imbalances, limit your consumption of seeds and nuts and include them in a varied diet rather than as the main source of food.

Eat calcium-rich foods, such as broccoli, dark leafy greens, and fortified foods, to help your lovebird's bones stay strong and prevent calcium deficiency. Mineral blocks and cuttlebones can also be provided as additional sources of calcium.

- Possible nutritional deficiencies:

Lovebirds may experience various health problems and inadequacies due to inadequate nutrition. Typical food shortages among romantic partners include:

Vitamin A deficiency: Immune system dysfunction, breathing difficulties, and visual abnormalities can result from a diet low in vitamin A. Make sure your lovebird eats plenty of foods rich in vitamin A, such as sweet potatoes, carrots and dark leafy greens.

Calcium deficiency: Lovebirds' bones and muscles depend on calcium for their proper functioning. Weak muscles, malformed bones, and fragile egg shells can all be symptoms of calcium deficiency. To avoid deficiencies, offer foods and supplements rich in calcium.

Vitamin D Deficiency: For general health and calcium absorption, lovebirds need vitamin D. To encourage vitamin D creation, make sure your lovebird has access to full-spectrum UVB lighting or natural sunlight. Serve foods rich in vitamin D, such as leafy greens and fortified pellets.

Protein Deficiency: Lovebirds need protein for general growth, tissue repair and muscle development. Make sure your lovebird eats enough protein-rich foods, such as eggs, lean meats, lentils and enriched pellets.

- Develop nutritious eating practices:

In order to promote optimal nutrition and avoid nutritional imbalances, it is imperative that you cultivate healthy eating habits in your loved one. Here are some tips for creating a healthy diet:

Offer a variety of foods: To promote acceptance and avoid picky eating habits, expose your sweetheart to a wide variety of foods from a young age. To keep things interesting and provide a variety of nutrients, rotate your foods frequently.

Keep an eye on portion proportions: overfeeding your lovebird can lead to obesity, which can lead to a number of health problems. So pay attention to portion proportions. Follow the dietary recommendations made based on the size, age and activity level of your lovebird.

Provide Clean, Fresh Water Every Day: To prevent dehydration and to support overall health, make sure your lovebird always has access to clean, fresh water. To stop bacterial growth, change the water daily and clean the water bowl frequently.

Control the intake of treats: Limit the amount of seeds, nuts and sweets you give your lovebird, as they can be high in calories and fat. Treats should be used sparingly and offered as an incentive for good behavior or as part of a healthy diet.

Promote Foraging: Give your lovebird the chance to engage in natural foraging activities by hiding food in puzzle feeders, foraging trays, or toys. Engaging in foraging activities encourages natural eating behaviors and increases mental and physical activity.

Maintaining your lovebird's general health, energy and longevity requires feeding them a good, balanced diet. You can ensure your lovebird gets the essential nutrients it needs to thrive by providing it with a wide range of foods, such as specially prepared pellets, fresh fruit and vegetables, cereals and occasional treats. To ensure your feathered companion has the best possible health and well-being, start your child with good eating habits and be aware of possible dietary deficiencies. You and your inseparable partner can have a long and fulfilling relationship if you provide them with the proper nourishment and care.

Chapter 4

Socializing and Bonding Tips for Lovebirds: Building a Strong Bond with Your Feathered Friend

An essential part of love for lovebirds is socializing and bonding. These perceptive and gregarious birds love companionship and engagement, from their partners to their human caretakers. Creating a close relationship with your lovebird improves both your experiences as a pet owner and your bird's quality of life. We'll review several bonding and socialization strategies for lovebirds in this detailed book, including ways to foster interaction, foster trust, and improve your lovebird's environment.

- Know the behavior of lovebirds:

Understanding the innate habits and social dynamics of lovebirds is crucial before diving into socialization and bonding tips. Lovebirds are gregarious birds that maintain strong pair relationships and participate in various social activities such as vocalizing, feeding, and preening. Lovebirds are animals that live in herds in the wild and depend on each other for mating, communication, and safety.

Lovebirds raised as pets frequently develop close relationships with their human guardians and need frequent social contact to thrive. But since every lovebird is different and has their own tastes and comfort zones, bonding and socialization should be approached with tolerance, understanding and respect.

- Establish trust:

Establishing trust is the cornerstone of a strong relationship with your significant other. Building trust takes time and requires tolerance, consistency and encouraging feedback. The following tips will help you develop trust with your sweetheart:

Respect their boundaries: Avoid pressuring your sweetheart in embarrassing circumstances and let him come to you on his own terms. Be attentive to their personal space and avoid surprising them with loud noises or sudden movements.

Offer rewards and candy: Reward desired actions, such as walking on your hand or perching on your shoulder, with candy. Your relationship with your inseparable is strengthened and good associations are formed thanks to positive reinforcement.

Spend quality time together: Set aside time each day to engage in calm, pleasant conversation with your sweetheart. Play with toys or explore their surroundings, gently massage their heads, touch them, and talk to them in a calm, soothing manner.

Be patient and consistent: Building trust with your partner takes time, so be patient and consistent when interacting with them. As your sweetheart comes to trust you, establish and maintain a schedule and offer comfort and encouragement along the way.

- Encourage communication:

Maintaining cerebral and emotional stimulation for your lovebird requires social bonding. The following tips can help you encourage communication with your sweetheart:

Provide plenty of opportunities for socialization: Invite your partner to participate in various activities around the house to promote socialization. Let them accompany you to work, watch TV, or play hobbies so you can spend time together and bond.

Offer enrichment activities: To occupy and amuse your lovebird, offer a range of toys, perches and enrichment activities. To avoid boredom and encourage play and exploration, alternate toys regularly.

Arrange play dates: To encourage socialization and companionship among your many lovebirds or other pet birds, arrange supervised play dates. Engaging in social interactions with other birds can provide significant opportunities for interaction and enrichment.

Imitate natural activities: To improve communication and strengthen your relationship with your lovebird, imitate natural activities like feeding, vocalizing, and preening. Give your lovebird some attention by brushing and preening its feathers, hand feeding it, and making soft sounds to show your attention.

- Improve your sweetheart's mood:

Improving your lovebird's environment is crucial if you want to encourage mental stimulation, exercise, and overall well-being. The following tips can help you improve your lovebird's environment:

Offer a Variety of Toys: To keep your lovebird occupied both mentally and physically, offer a varied assortment of toys, such as swings, bells, ropes, and chew toys. Toys should be rotated frequently to encourage exploration and avoid boredom.

Provide foraging opportunities: By hiding food and treats in toys, foraging trays or puzzle feeders, you can promote natural foraging behaviors. Engaging in foraging activities gives your lovebird significant enrichment while also promoting mental and physical activity.

Provide natural wood perches and branches: To promote good foot health and prevent foot problems, provide natural wood perches and branches in a range of sizes. Sandpaper and rough textured perches should not be used as they may cause abrasions and discomfort.

Give your lovebird access to natural sunlight: Give your lovebird access to natural sunlight and fresh air by allowing him to spend time outside in a safe, supervised setting. Sun exposure improves vitamin D creation, helps people maintain a healthy circadian rhythm, and generally improves their health and well-being.

- Safety observations:

When you socialize and bond with your lovebird, you have an obligation to keep them safe. Here are some crucial safety factors to remember:

Supervise interactions: To avoid any incidents or conflicts, be sure to constantly keep an eye on the interactions between your lovebird and other pets, including cats and dogs. When you are not there, keep other animals away from your lovebird's cage.

Avoid Toxic Compounds: To avoid inadvertent ingestion or exposure, eliminate all toxic compounds from your lovebird's environment, including pesticides, household chemicals, and toxic plants.

Keep an eye out for signals of tension: Monitor your lovebird's behavior and body language for cues of tension or discomfort, such as fluffy feathers, rapid breathing, or a combative posture. Eliminate all possible sources of tension and offer consolation and assistance if necessary.

Practice gentle handling: Do not grab or chain your lovebird forcefully; Instead, treat them gently. To develop confidence in handling, use gradual desensitization procedures and positive reinforcement.

In summary:

In order to properly care for lovebirds and establish a strong, reliable bond with your feathered friend, socialization and bonding are crucial. You can create a supportive and exciting environment in which your lovebird can thrive by being aware of their natural habits, giving them plenty of opportunities to socialize, improving their environment, and making sure they are safe at all times . Remember to interact with your lovebird with patience, consistency and respect, and enjoy the fulfilling feeling of creating a lasting relationship with your feathered companion.

Chapter 5

Know the behavior of lovebirds

Lovebirds are enchanting birds distinguished by their vibrant feathers, lively activities, and close social bonds. In order to properly care for lovebirds, beautify their environment and foster harmonious relationships with their human companions, it is imperative to understand their behavior. We'll delve into the complex realm of lovebird behavior in this detailed guide, covering topics like their innate tendencies, social interactions, communication patterns, and typical behavior patterns.

- Natural habits and instincts:

Similar to other parrot species, lovebirds display an array of innate instincts and behaviors that are deeply rooted in their evolutionary past. Lovebirds have developed certain habits to help them live long and prosperous lives in their natural environment. Some of the essential innate tendencies and actions of lovebirds include:

Preening: Lovebirds use their beaks to clean and preserve their feathers while preening, an important grooming behavior. Preening keeps feathers healthy and promotes waterproofing by helping to remove dirt, debris and parasites.

Foraging lovebirds, which is normal behavior, search and collect food in their environment. Lovebirds spend a lot of time searching for seeds, fruits, insects, and other food sources when in the wild. Giving them the chance to feed in captivity satisfies their innate inclinations and stimulates their minds.

Lovebirds are noisy animals that use a range of noises and vocalizations to communicate, such as whistles, chirps, screams, and melodic calls. Vocalizations are essential for sexual attractiveness, territorial defense and social communication.

Nesting: To prepare for mating and raising young, breeding pairs of lovebirds adopt nesting behavior. To strengthen their pair bond and prepare for childbearing, lovebirds build nests from twigs, leaves, and other materials. They also participate in courtship rituals.

Lovebirds are gregarious birds that inhabit their natural habitats in groups. Lovebirds that gather together are better able to find food sources, protect themselves from predators, and remain a cohesive group. Lovebirds kept in captivity may display herding behavior, such as seeking out other birds to socialize with or developing close relationships with their human caretakers.

- Social structure:

Lovebirds are gregarious birds that bond well in pairs with their partners and participate in a range of social activities within their flock or human family. Giving lovebirds the social engagement and companionship they need to thrive requires an understanding of their social dynamics. The key elements of the social dynamics of lovebirds are:

Lovebirds are monogamous avians who establish lasting pair bonds with their partners. Once mated, lovebirds mate for life and maintain their relationship by preening, feeding, and vocalizing to each other.

Lovebirds tend to be territorial, especially during mating season when they protect their nesting site and the surrounding area from strangers. When kept in captivity, lovebirds may become territorial and protect their cage or favorite perch from intruders.

Dominance and submission can be used by lovebirds to create hierarchy within their flock or social group. Submissive birds may engage in appeasement behaviors, such as grooming or avoiding conflict, while dominant birds may demonstrate aggressive behaviors, such as lunging, chasing, or vocalizing, to establish dominance.

Socialization: Lovebirds are gregarious birds that enjoy companionship and interaction. They depend on social interactions for mating, communication, and safety in their large herds seen in the wild. To avoid loneliness and boredom, lovebirds in captivity benefit from socializing with other birds or human friends.

- Communication techniques :

A key part of lovebirds' behavior is communication, which allows them to share information, express feelings, and maintain social connections. Lovebirds communicate with each other and their human guardians in several ways. Typical means of communication are:

Lovebirds are talkative animals that communicate with a wide variety of noises and vocalizations. Depending on the situation and the feeling, these vocalizations can have different tones, pitches and intensities. Lovebirds can communicate their happiness, joy, fear or hostility through vocalizations.

Lovebirds use a variety of postures, gestures and movements to convey messages through their body language. For example, when a lovebird senses danger, it may fluff its feathers to appear larger and more threatening or hunker down to express fear or abandonment.

Lovebirds have expressive faces capable of expressing a multitude of feelings and intentions. Their facial expressions for communicating with other birds or their human caregivers may include eye pinching, beak grinding, and head bobbing.

Lovebirds may converse with each other or visually convey their intentions by flapping their wings, wagging their tails, or tilting their heads. Their intentions, social status, and mood can all be inferred from these visual cues.

- Typical behavior patterns:

Lovebirds exhibit a range of behavioral behaviors typical of their species. You will be able to better understand your lovebird's behavior and meet their needs by being aware of these tendencies. Typical activity patterns of lovebirds are as follows:

Nesting Behavior: During the breeding season, lovebirds may engage in activities related to nest building, such as gathering materials, shredding paper, and building nests. Giving them a nest box or appropriate nesting material will help them satisfy their innate desires and stop unwanted behavior.

Aggression: When feeling threatened or defending their territory, lovebirds may act aggressively by biting, lunging, or making territorial displays. Aggressive behavior can be reduced by being aware of the factors that lead to violence and creating a calm and predictable atmosphere.

Playfulness: Lovebirds are lively animals that enjoy participating in a variety of activities, including interacting with their human partners, playing with toys, and exploring their surroundings. To meet their needs for physical and mental stimulation, provide them with an abundance of toys, perches and enrichment activities.

Lovebirds are talkative birds that take great pleasure in talking and interacting with other members of their flock or human family. Although lovebirds vocalize naturally, excessive vocalization can be a sign of tension, boredom, or loneliness. Reducing excessive vocalizations can be achieved by providing plenty of social connection, enrichment, and mental stimulation.

Understanding lovebird behavior is crucial to providing them with appropriate care, improving their environment, and establishing a strong, reliable bond with their human friends. You can better meet their demands and ensure their health and well-being by being aware of their typical behaviors, communication styles, social dynamics and innate inclinations. You can have a happy and fulfilling connection with your feathered friend for many years if you demonstrate patience, empathy and a better understanding of lovebird behavior.

Chapter 6

Caring for the health and well-being of your lovebirds to ensure their longevity and contentment

Your lovebird's longevity, happiness, and overall well-being depend on your ability to care for their health and well-being. Lovebirds need routine care, attention and preventative measures to stay healthy and avoid illness, just like any other pet. We'll cover a wide range of topics related to lovebird health care and wellness in this comprehensive book, including feeding and nutrition, potty training and grooming, environmental factors, common health problems, and care. preventive veterinarians.

- Nutrition and diet:

For lovebirds, a healthy diet is the cornerstone of good health. Vitality, a robust immune system and overall health are all supported by a balanced diet, which offers essential nutrients, vitamins and minerals. Here are some important things to consider when feeding your lovebird a healthy diet:

Formulated Pellets: A convenient, well-balanced food source, premium pellets are specially designed for lovebirds. To support your lovebird's overall health, look for pellets enriched with vitamins, minerals and amino acids.

Fresh fruits and vegetables: To improve your lovebird's diet, offer a range of fresh fruits and vegetables. Vegetables like leafy greens, carrots, peppers and broccoli provide essential nutrients and hydration, while fruits like apples, bananas, grapes and strawberries are rich in fiber, vitamins and antioxidants. .

Nuts and Seeds: Although you can give your lovebird occasional treats like seeds and nuts, they should not make up the majority of his diet. To avoid weight and nutritional imbalances, limit your consumption of seeds and nuts and include them in a varied diet rather than as the main source of food.

Calcium and Vitamin D: To maintain bone health and avoid deficiencies, make sure your lovebird's diet contains sufficient amounts of these two nutrients. To encourage vitamin D creation, serve calcium-rich meals, such as broccoli, dark leafy greens, and fortified foods, and give them access to full-spectrum UVB lamps or natural sunlight.

- Grooming and hygiene:

Maintaining good grooming and hygiene habits is essential to keeping your lovebird healthy and comfortable . Here are some important grooming and hygiene tips:

Bathing: To maintain healthy and clean feathers, lovebirds like to take baths. To encourage the bathing habit, provide your lovebird with a shallow dish of water or mist it with a spray bottle. Shampoo and soap can strip the natural oils from their feathers, so avoid using them.

Regular nail trimming is essential to keep your lovebird comfortable and prevent overgrowth. Trim the tips of their nails with pet-safe nail clippers or files, taking care not to cut the fast-moving blood vessel inside the nail.

Beak Maintenance: Lovebirds chew and bite toys and perches, which naturally wears out their beaks. For advice on how to properly care for your lovebird's beak , talk to a veterinarian if you notice overgrowth or abnormalities.

Caring for feathers: Check your lovebird's feathers frequently for damage, feathering, or molting. Give them plenty of opportunities to groom and preen, and make sure their environment is free of drafts and high humidity, as these elements could harm the health of their feathers.

- Environmental factors to consider

Ensuring the safety and comfort of your lovebird is crucial to promoting their overall health and well-being. The following environmental factors should be remembered:

Cage Setup: Make sure your lovebird has plenty of space to walk around, spread its wings, and exercise in a spacious, well-ventilated cage. Provide them with toys, swings and enrichment activities to keep them engaged both cognitively and physically, as well as a variety of sizes and textures of cots.

Cage Location: Keep the cage in a quiet, serene part of your home, away from drafts, sunlight and any potential dangers. To prevent them from becoming stressed or anxious, make sure the cage is at eye level and gives them a good view of their surroundings.

Temperature and Humidity: Lovebirds are sensitive to changes in both the former and the latter. To avoid heat exhaustion or breathing problems, keep the temperature comfortably between 65 and 80 degrees Fahrenheit and the humidity between 40 and 60 percent.

Safety Tips: Get rid of anything that could endanger your lovebird, including household chemicals, electrical cords, poisonous plants, and sharp objects. Make sure all doors and windows are securely closed to avoid accidents or leaks.

- Typical health problems:

Even though lovebirds are generally tough and resilient birds, there are a number of health issues that can negatively impact their well-being. Understanding common health problems and their symptoms will allow you to spot problems early and take appropriate action. Some of the health problems that lovebirds often face include:

Lovebirds are susceptible to respiratory illnesses, which can be caused by bacteria, viruses or fungi. Lethargy, difficulty breathing, runny nose, sneezing and wheezing are possible symptoms. Veterinary care must be provided quickly to avoid difficulties.

Gastrointestinal Conditions: Crop stasis, or the slowing or impaction of crops, is one of the gastrointestinal conditions that lovebirds are susceptible to, along with vomiting and diarrhea. Improper eating habits, bacterial infections, or underlying medical conditions can all contribute to these problems. For an accurate diagnosis and treatment, talk to a veterinarian.

Feather Plucking: Lovebirds that engage in excessive grooming or plucking of their feathers may have behavioral problems that cause bald patches and skin irritations. Stress, boredom, environmental causes, or underlying health conditions can all contribute to feather plucking. Feather plucking can be stopped by treating the underlying cause and providing enrichment and mental stimulation.

External parasites like lice and mites can infest lovebirds, causing damage to their feathers as well as irritated and itchy skin. You can prevent infestations and maintain the health of your lovebird by performing routine inspections and treating it with the appropriate pest control treatments.

- Veterinary preventive care:

The health and well-being of your lovebird depends on routine veterinary exams. A licensed avian veterinarian can perform routine exams, offer preventative treatment, and manage any emerging health issues. Here are some essential elements of preventative veterinary care for lovebirds:

Wellness Checks: To keep an eye on your lovebird's health and identify any possible problems early, schedule routine wellness checkups with a licensed avian veterinarian. The veterinarian will physically examine your lovebird, assess its environment and diet, and make preventative care recommendations during a wellness exam.

Diagnostic Tests: To determine your lovebird's general health and check for any potential health problems, diagnostic tests such as blood tests, fecal exams, or imaging exams may occasionally be advised. Proper treatment can be guided by diagnostic tests, which can help identify underlying problems.

vaccinations: To protect against avian polyomavirus and psittacine beak and feather disease (PBFD), among other viral diseases, some lovebirds may benefit from vaccinations. Depending on your lovebird's lifestyle and risk factors, talk to your avian veterinarian to see if vaccinations are recommended.

Nutritional Advice: To ensure that your lovebird receives a well-balanced, nutrient-rich diet, a qualified avian veterinarian can offer sound nutritional advice and dietary recommendations. Nutritional counseling can help prevent obesity, dietary deficiencies and other diet-related health problems.

It takes diligence, attention to detail, and a proactive approach to preventative care to maintain the health and well-being of your lovebird. Your lovebird can live a long, happy, healthy life if you feed him a balanced diet, groom him well, create a safe and comfortable environment, watch for common health problems, and schedule regular veterinary checkups. Always keep a watchful eye out for any behavioral or physical changes in your lovebird, and do not hesitate to seek prompt veterinary attention if you have any concerns about their health or well-being. You can have a happy and fulfilling relationship with your feathered companion for many years if you give it proper care and attention.

Chapter 7

Training methods for lovers

The enjoyable experience of training a lovebird not only enriches and stimulates your mind, but also improves the bond between you and your feathered friend. Lovebirds are gregarious and intelligent birds that learn positive reinforcement methods well. You can teach your lovebird a range of actions and commands that improve its quality of life and promote harmonious connection if you are patient, consistent and understanding. We'll review a variety of lovebird training methods in this comprehensive book, including procedures for teaching basic commands, managing behavior problems, and encouraging good interactions.

- Understand the fundamentals of training:

The fundamentals of successful bird training must be understood before delving into particular training methods. To train your lovebird to perform desired actions and discourage unwanted actions, you will need to be patient, consistent, and provide positive reinforcement. Here are some key ideas to remember:

Positive reinforcement: To encourage repetition of desired behaviors, positive reinforcement involves offering treats, praise, or other rewards. To encourage your darling to voluntarily engage in desired activities and establish good associations, reinforce them without delay.

Consistency: Training performance depends on maintaining consistency. Maintain consistency in your teaching strategies, cues, and prompts to avoid misunderstandings and successfully reinforce desired behavior. To achieve the results you want, set clear expectations and deliver on them consistently.

Patience is a virtue when training, especially with lovebirds who may have different preferences and paces. When dealing with your sweetheart, show patience and empathy; don't rush them or make them do something they don't feel comfortable doing.

Timing: In order to strengthen the association between the desired behavior and the reward, rewards must be distributed as soon as the behavior is achieved. This makes timing crucial in training. Mark the desired behavior with a clicker or verbal marker, then immediately give a reward.

- Fundamental training methods:

Establishing clear communication and providing basic instructions and actions to your lovebird will create the foundation for more advanced training. Here are some basic training methods to get you started:

Target training: This involves teaching your lovebird to use its beak to touch a specified object, such as a stick or finger. To begin, place the target next to your lovebird and when he touches it with his beak, offer him a treat or a compliment. Gradually increase the length and distance of the behavior until your lovebird consistently hits the target when cued.

Step-Up Command: When given, this command will cause your lovebird to walk on your finger or hand. Encourage your lovebird to walk on your hand by giving it a treat or gently moving its paws with your fingers. Hold your hand or finger near their feet and give a voice signal like "step up." Give them a reward immediately if they follow the signal.

Callback training: This technique trains your sweetheart to answer your calls. To start, call your sweetheart's name or use a specific reminder cue, such as a whistle or the phrase "come here." Treat your lovebird or use a target stick to direct it towards you, to make it fly or walk towards you. When they contact you, show them lots of gratitude.

With the help of harness training, you can take your lovebird on safe, supervised outdoor excursions. Before trying to put on the harness, introduce it gradually and give your lovebird time to explore and get used to it. Offer your lovebird a treat when he wears the harness and gradually extend his wearing time.

- Managing behavior problems:

Behavioral problems common in lovebirds, such as biting, screaming, or territorial behavior, can also be addressed with training. The following training methods can be used to resolve behavior problems:

Biting: It is important to identify the underlying cause of your lovebird's biting habit and take steps to remedy it. Encourage gentle interactions between beaks and minimize biting by using positive reinforcement tactics. When your lovebird tries to bite, focus on a toy or treat and praise him for his delicate beak interactions.

Yelling: Yelling too loudly or excessively may indicate boredom, attention-seeking behavior, or tension. By providing plenty of brain stimulation, social contact, and environmental enrichment, you can address the underlying reason. Reward calm behavior with positive reinforcement; ignore or deflect the screams.

Lovebirds can act territorially, especially near their cage or favorite perches. Give your lovebird plenty of opportunities for socialization and enrichment outside of his cage, and encourage him to explore new areas of his environment. To encourage calm, non-aggressive behavior, use positive reinforcement.

Fear and Hostility: Train your lovebird with patience and empathy if he shows signs of fear or hostility toward you or other family members. Use counterconditioning and desensitization strategies to gradually reduce anxiety and promote confidence. Over time, gradually increase the amount of exposure starting with low-stress interactions.

- Interactive and enriching training:

You can provide your sweetheart with opportunities for social connection, physical activity, and mental stimulation by including enrichment and interactive training in their regular routine. Here are some suggestions for interactive training and enrichments:

Puzzle Toys: Give your lovebirds puzzle toys, interactive feeders, and foraging toys to help them solve their problems and promote their natural foraging habits. To encourage your sweetheart to investigate and interact with the toys, hide food or treats inside.

Teach your sweetheart fun and enjoyable tricks, like shaking, spinning, and pretending to be dead. Each tip should be broken down into manageable steps and success should be rewarded with positive reinforcement. To keep your lovebird interested and motivated, keep training sessions brief and fun.

Establish a safe indoor flying zone for your darling so he can strengthen and exercise his flying muscles. This is called indoor flight training. To encourage your lovebird to fly to certain perches or targets, use positive reinforcement. When your lovebird flies successfully, give it food or praise.

Socialization Opportunities: Arrange supervised play dates with other birds or give your lovebird the opportunity to socialize with family members and guests. Positive social behaviors are encouraged and loneliness and boredom are alleviated through socialization.

The experience of training a lovebird is rewarding and enriching, strengthening the bond between you and your feathered friend and providing brain stimulation and enrichment. You and your lovebird can have a rewarding and beneficial training experience if you understand training principles, teach basic commands, manage behavior problems, and include enrichment and interactive training in your lovebird's daily routine.

Always be understanding, persistent and patient, and remember to recognize and appreciate each small victory as it comes. You and your inseparable companion can experience a lifelong adventure of growth and learning with commitment and effort.

Chapter 8

Fun Lovebird Enrichment Ideas and Activities: Improving Their Lives Through Play and Exploration

For lovebirds to be happy and healthy, they need to be cognitively and physically occupied. Entertaining your feathered friends and providing them with enrichment opportunities not only keeps them from getting bored, but also helps improve your relationship with them. We'll look at a wide range of enjoyable activities and enrichment suggestions in this detailed guide to keeping your lovebirds occupied, stimulated and happy.

- Know the behavior of lovebirds:

It's important to understand lovebirds' behavior and preferences before embarking on specific activities and enrichment ideas. Lovebirds are gregarious, intellectual and curious animals who enjoy companionship, learning and brain stimulation. They enjoy participating in activities like playing, exploring, and foraging that resemble natural behaviors. Understanding your lovebird's innate tendencies and preferences can help you tailor enrichment activities to meet their specific needs.

- Fun tasks and ideas for improvement:

Treats and toys from foraging:

Treat balls, puzzle feeders, and foraging boxes are examples of foraging toys that can be used to hide rewards or favorite meals. To stimulate your lovebirds' natural foraging instincts and problem-solving skills, encourage them to explore and manipulate toys to reveal hidden rewards.

Using safe materials like paper cups, cardboard tubes, or paper bags, make your own homemade foraging toys. Fill them with leftover food, shredded paper, or small candies, and watch how much your lovers enjoy the task of discovering the hidden treats.

Attractive games and toys:
Treat your lovers to a range of interactive games and toys to keep them busy and happy. Toys that promote play, discovery and physical activity include bells, swings, ladders and mirrors.

Engage your lovers in interactive games like pretend play, hide-and-seek, and hide-and-seek. Engage your lovebirds in conversation and encourage them to participate in activities using toys or your hands.

Practice and technique sessions:
Teach your lovers fun and enjoyable skills like fetch, twist and wiggle. Break each tip into manageable steps

and when someone tries it successfully, use positive reinforcement strategies like praise and treats.

Include training sessions in your daily schedule to foster relationships and mental stimulation. To keep your lovebirds interested and motivated, keep your training sessions short, sweet and upbeat.

Environmental investigation:
Give your lovers an exciting and comfortable space to explore and learn. Provide a range of perches, branches and climbing frames to encourage movement and organic activities.

To maintain an attractive and novel environment for your lovebirds, turn over toys, perches and cage accessories regularly. To excite their senses and spark their interest, introduce them to different toys, materials and textures.

- Outdoor excursions:

Take your sweethearts on supervised outdoor excursions to expose them to new sights, sounds and air. For outdoor adventures, make sure they are safe by using a secure carrier or harness.

Provide your lovebirds with a secure outdoor aviary or playpen where they can enjoy the outdoors without fear of predators or other dangers. Provide branches, perches and other organic components to make your outdoor space attractive.

- Connections and socialization:

Arrange supervised play dates with other paired birds or let your lovebirds socialize with family members and guests. Opportunities for socialization reduce loneliness and boredom and encourage sociable behavior.

Spend time playing, grooming, and gently handling your lovebirds to strengthen your bond. Talk gently to them, give them a gentle pat on the head, and engage in enjoyable activities like exploring or playing with toys.

- Intense perception:

Offer your lovers a range of sensory experiences to pique their interest. Offer them toys that vary in texture, color and shape to stimulate their tactile and visual senses.

For your lovers, create a relaxing and enriching environment by playing relaxing music or nature sounds. Try a variety of noises and see how your lovebirds react to help you understand what they like.

- Handmade toys and projects:

Use your imagination to create safe, non-toxic homemade toys and enrichment activities for your lovers. There are endless opportunities for fun and discovery when working on craft creations like fruit kabob skewers, cardboard forts, and paper shredders.

Allow loved ones to help you shred paper, tear cardboard, or skewer fruit to add a little love to your DIY project. Participating in hands-on activities with your feathered friends helps deepen your relationship with them.

- Puzzle solving difficulties:

Puzzle solutions and enrichment activities will test your lovebirds' problem-solving skills. Provide puzzle toys that require your lovers to manipulate objects in order to access treats or incentives, like interactive mazes or food-dispensing balls.

As your lovers get better at solving problems, gradually increase the difficulty level to provide them with mental stimulation and a sense of accomplishment.

- Engaging meals:

Use interactive eating approaches to make mealtimes more interesting and educational. To stimulate natural foraging habits, scatter food or treats throughout the cage or hide them in foraging toys.

Use your imagination to display fresh produce in interesting ways, such as hanging it from the ceiling of the cage or skewering lush fruits and green vegetables. Try various presentation techniques to bring excitement and variety to meals.

Engaging games and enrichment ideas are essential for keeping lovebirds mentally and physically stimulated, improving their overall health and well-being, and strengthening your relationship with your feathered friends. You can provide your lovebirds with opportunities for play, exploration and socialization that resemble their natural environments and behaviors by introducing a range of enrichment activities into their daily routine. To create enriching experiences specific to the needs and preferences of each of your lovebirds, use your imagination, try various activities, and be attentive to their preferences. You can give your loved ones a rich and meaningful life full of adventure, excitement and unlimited possibilities if you put in effort, are creative and have a spirit of dedication.

Chapter 9

Common Myths About Dissident Lovebirds: Differentiating Fact From Fiction

The lovebirds' vibrant plumage, lively activities and close social bonds have won over bird lovers around the world. But like many other well-known pets, lovebirds are frequently the subject of myths and false beliefs, which can cause misunderstandings regarding their requirements, temperament and level of care. We'll dispel popular lovebird lore and offer factual facts in this comprehensive guide to help you better understand and care for these endearing bird friends.

Myth 1: For lovebirds to thrive, they must be kept in pairs

Factual Statement: Although lovebirds are gregarious birds that form close pair relationships with their partners, they do not always need a partner to survive in captivity. Lovebirds that receive enough mental stimulation, social interaction, and companionship can develop close relationships with their human guardians and lead happy lives on their own. To avoid loneliness and boredom, you need to spend a lot of time engaging with your lonely lovebird and providing enrichment activities if you decide to keep one.

Myth 2: Small cages are suitable for keeping lovebirds

Factual Statement: Lovebirds are gregarious, feisty birds that need plenty of space to roam, spread their wings, and exercise. Despite their small size, lovebirds need large cages with plenty of room to perch, fly short distances, and engage in their natural foraging and exploring activities. For a single lovebird, a cage at least

24 inches by 24 inches by 24 inches is recommended, with additional space needed for each additional bird.

Myth 3: You can only give seeds to lovebirds

Factual Statement: Although seeds can be a popular treat for parrots, they should not make up the bulk of their diet. A diet limited to seeds is low in vitamins, minerals and other essential nutrients and can lead to obesity, nutritional deficiencies and other health problems. A range of fresh fruit and vegetables, leafy greens, pellets and sometimes seeds and nuts as treats are all part of a lovebird's healthy diet. A balanced diet ensures that lovebirds have all the nutrients they need to stay healthy and happy.

Myth 4: Low-maintenance animals are lovebirds

Factual Statement: To live in captivity, lovebirds require constant care, attention and commitment. They are gregarious and intellectual birds that need mental and physical exercise as well as socialization opportunities to avoid becoming bored and developing behavioral problems. Lovebirds need to be fed, cleaned and socialized every day. They should also have regular veterinary check-ups to ensure they remain healthy. Lovebirds need plenty of social engagement, enrichment activities, and a vibrant environment to meet their needs and maintain their health.

Myth 5: Long-term alone time isn't bad for lovebirds

Factual Statement: Lovebirds are gregarious animals that need daily companionship to avoid boredom and loneliness. Long-term isolation of lovebirds can cause stress, anxiety, and behavioral problems, including vocalizations, aggression, and feather plucking. Arrange for a reliable pet sitter or sitter to care for your loved ones while you are away if you need to spend an extended period of time away from home. Alternatively, to keep your lovebirds company while you are away, consider adopting a pet bird.

Myth 6: Silent animals are lovebirds

Factual Statement: Although lovebirds are smaller than some other parrot species, they can still make loud vocalizations, especially early in the morning and late in the evening. Vocalizations are used by lovebirds to establish territory, convey feelings, and communicate with other members of their flock. Lovebirds can make noisy pets although they are not as loud as larger parrot species, especially when stressed, bored or nervous. A regular daily schedule, plenty of mental stimulation, and social interactions can reduce excessive vocalizations in lovebirds.

Myth 7: Raising lovebirds is easy

Factual Statement: To ensure the health and well-being of birds and their offspring, raising lovebirds requires meticulous planning, preparation and dedication. As monogamous birds that develop close bonds with their partners, lovebirds require suitable partners, appropriate nesting environments, and ongoing care to ensure successful reproduction. Raising lovebirds can also be physically and emotionally taxing, requiring close observation of the breeding pair, eggs and chicks to ensure their health and well-being. It is important to learn about breeding practices, speak with avian veterinarians or experienced breeders, and be prepared for the obligations and difficulties of raising lovebirds before attempting to breed them.

Myth 8: There is no need for veterinary care for lovebirds

Fact: To maintain their health and well-being, lovebirds, like all pets, must receive routine veterinary care. To keep an eye on your lovebird's overall health, quickly identify any possible health issues, and administer preventative care such as vaccinations and pest control, routine checkups with an avian veterinarian are crucial. Lovebirds are also good at hiding symptoms of illness, so it's important to keep an eye out for any changes in behavior, appetite, or appearance that might indicate a medical problem. To treat health issues and ensure the best possible outcome for your lovebird, prompt veterinary care is essential.

Myth 9: Children can adopt lovebirds as pets

Fact: Although lovebirds can make delightful pets for responsible, mature children under adult supervision, they may not be suitable for young children or households with inexperienced caregivers. Lovebirds are delicate little birds that require gentle handling and respect for their boundaries. They can be easily startled or injured by rough handling, loud noises or sudden movements. Additionally, lovebirds have sharp beaks and claws that can cause injury if mishandled. Before bringing a lovebird into a home with children, it is essential to educate children on the proper care and handling of birds and supervise interactions between children and birds to ensure safety and well-being of both parties.

Myth 10: Lovebirds don't need toys or enrichment

Fact: Lovebirds are intelligent, active birds that require mental stimulation and enrichment to avoid boredom and behavioral problems. Providing a variety of toys, perches and enrichment activities is essential to keeping lovebirds mentally and physically stimulated. Toys such as bells, swings, ladders, foraging toys and puzzle feeders provide opportunities for play, exploration and problem solving. Periodically rotating toys and introducing new toys and activities keeps your lovebirds active and minimizes boredom. Additionally, providing opportunities for social interaction, flight exercise, and outdoor exploration further enriches your lovebirds' lives and promotes their overall well-being.

Lovebirds are intriguing and charismatic birds that bring fun and companionship to their human caregivers. By debunking common myths and misconceptions about lovebirds, we can better understand their needs, behavior and care requirements. By providing accurate information and responsible care, lovebirds receive the attention, enrichment and companionship they need to thrive in captivity. With proper care, understanding and respect for their unique personalities, lovebirds can live fulfilling and enriching lives as valued members of the family.

Printed in Dunstable, United Kingdom